Amends

poems by

Cindy Day

Finishing Line Press
Georgetown, Kentucky

Amends

for Ray who supported me all the way

Copyright © 2016 by Cindy Day
ISBN 978-1-63534-041-9 First Edition
All rights reserved under International and Pan-American Copyright Conventions.
No part of this book may be reproduced in any manner whatsoever without written permission from the publisher, except in the case of brief quotations embodied in critical articles and reviews.

ACKNOWLEDGMENTS

These poems have never been published. They were all written during my three years at the Downtown Writer's Center in Syracuse NY. I cannot thank the writers at DWC enough for their support, especially Phil Memmer, Georgia Popoff, Jesse Nissim, Eric Berlin, Jennifer Glancy, Susan Charlton, Judy Carr, Carol Biesemeyer, and Andrew Schep. And here at home, special thanks to Vige Barrie, Margie Thickston, and Susan Schafer.

Publisher: Leah Maines

Editor: Christen Kincaid

Cover Art: Vige Barrie

Author Photo: Ray Bepko

Cover Design: Elizabeth Maines

Printed in the USA on acid-free paper.
Order online: www.finishinglinepress.com
　　　　　also available on amazon.com

　　　　　　　　Author inquiries and mail orders:
　　　　　　　　　　Finishing Line Press
　　　　　　　　　　　P. O. Box 1626
　　　　　　　　　Georgetown, Kentucky 40324
　　　　　　　　　　　　U. S. A.

Table of Contents

Dobbs at Great Bend 1
Future Me 3
Shadow 4
Little Human 5
Join the Others 6
Plans Are for Others 7
The Younger Generation 11
We Skinny Kids 12
Fear is a Story 13
The Red House, Late March 14
Beaujolais 18
A Death in the Other House 19
White August 20
The Visitors 22
Fearless Moral Inventory 23
Finding My Way to Jesus 25
Amends 26
Amends 2 27
The Sacred Tables 28

The cause of alcoholism is unknown.

Merck Manual 1992

Dobbs at Great Bend

Named for a bend in the Susquehana,
Great Bend is where I pause,
feel the freight of life Upstate
fall away behind me,
the return to my family in the South begin.

My mother, asleep in her hospital bed,
is down to small rituals,
meals, the bathroom,
one daughter, one son.

Twice a year, sometimes more,
I drive from my present into my past,
out of my past into my present,
telling myself it will never come clear,
praying it will, for words I don't have.

I stop at Dobbs in Great Bend
because I like the coffee, the climate
of resignation, old wooden tables
and greasy white plates.

I wish my only task is to carry a heavy tray
and not figure out how to stay sober.
I wonder why what is clear to others
isn't clear to me. Did their mothers
speak magic words? "She did the best she could
with what she had," my sponsor says.

I sit in my booth preparing for the distance
between us, for gossip about my aunts
and the nurses, for the moment when
she slowly turns her head, her voice
strained to its highest pitch,
and asks if I am still writing poetry.

I stare at the mountains rising south of Great Bend
and grow aware of my sin and disposition.
Heading north again, the same mountains
subsiding into the state of New York,
I practice lowering my expectations.

It is all like cars without seat belts,
but I am on my way to meet her,
to another chance not to quarrel.
That is, I choose not to
and she can do whatever she wants.

Future Me

The loneliness came later. I was about ten
  and slowed my bike
on the hill above our house—like coming upon
  an ocean—

a look at the sides and corners, the black roof,
  the windows in my room
staring out at me, at my weight and the bike's
  resting on

my right foot. Many times my parents told us
  we would grow up
like them and move away and now I saw
  the place

I couldn't stay, would somehow leave and never
  see again, or see
from the outside only. The thought of her,
  the future me,

straightened my back. I kicked the kick stand up
  and set the bike
flying down the hill, leaning hard into the right
  turn home.

Shadow

The loneliness remains silent, even to her, for years.
Her secret, her shadow alongside her at school
and on the way home in buses and carpools.

Quiet surrounds her, a force field
the others bounce off of.

She takes it to mean, she imagines
she's ugly, odd, something
is wrong with her hair, her shirt.

The silence of her room, the softness of her bed,
the window on the road, the door she can close—
this is the place she can undress
and her shadow can rest.

Little Human

I am a small person ferried room to room,
not a child. My mother
carries me down the shady streets
and crowded avenues,

a little human, wordless
but aware there, close to her breast,
of her smell, the feel of her coat,
the rhythms of her breath;

of her curse on all of it,
kitchen, the dinner she doesn't want to make,
friends she doesn't want to see,
the man she tires of, the dreamy one
she might have had.

Now stuck with me, her own small self,
her idiot, mouth open, staring out
the car windows.

Join the Others

A car full of kids, a drive to the beach at Madison
with Judy's mother, shoulder to jiggling shoulder,
one silly story after another,

carols of laughter, barrettes and hats falling off,
a pinch, a howl, a good-natured punch back,
the car doors burst open

and they run toward the sand, the red umbrellas,
the cascading blues and whites, and shake their towels out
in no time

as the last girl out of the car shows up,
walking jerkily, her feet sinking, pushing crosswise
into the sand.

They are already in the water. "Go on now,"
says Judy's mother, "go on and join the others."
It is an order

she has often heard and always obeyed, never
without wishing the waters would recede,
or the others drown;

wondering why there isn't another choice,
why being herself
is wrong.

Plans Are for Others

1
They always arrive together
and I come late.
And I am late.

They are born into their clothes,
the way the collars open and sleeves fall.
They wear their shirts like they don't care

about their shirts, or just found them
on the floor. Same with their hair.
Like they just found it on their heads.

Keds thudding down the embankment,
they run onto the center field,
the one place I never go. This

is what I wear like they wear their hair
and their sweats: the defense
and the bench. The bench,

much as I dislike the passive voice,
is where I was placed after some long ago
Darwinian failure to catch or kick

the ball; where it was decided I would stand
at the goal but never cross it, defend
but never enter it.

2
In the afternoons she drives a few miles
to LaSalles, her lists folded
in her pocket,

careful lists she made at the kitchen table
after counting eggs and searching
empty spaces.

Market shelves piled with cereal
and apples cheer her and she fills
three or four bags with her list

and what meets her eye,
boxes and jars promising
happy families, prizes, smooth intestines.

Driving home she feels a little full.
How will she cook all this?
What will she turn it into?

The quiet street is even quieter
as if, like her, preparing
for the children to come home

full of crazy little stories
and that smell of sunlight and dirt.
Maybe she's the crazy one.

She thinks about that a lot.
The light grows dull in the living room
but she likes it that way, leaves the lamps

off, cold little statues.
She thinks about dinner again, clings to it
like a raft in waves

of time. Pork chops and baked potato.
After the children he comes, like the dark.
She stays in the kitchen,

the room he never enters except to pass through,
and heats up the pan. The kids are hungry.
When, they want to know.

How long? What? Pork chops, she tells them.
Just a second. Soon. Coming. It will all be over
in ten minutes.

3
Years later Kate begged me to take her
to the State Fair and I promised.
But as we grew near the acres

of parked cars, the mob of jiggling
asses, shuttle buses, popped corn,
I chickened out.

"I can't," I said to her small eager face,
 knowing full well what
 such happiness felt like when it was lost.

Ours was a flimsy race. How many times
had we heard I'll be there
only to arrive like Kate at the Fair,

our helpless joy and empty stomachs
transposed into a mystery, a hidden fear;
or reworked into a rationale

for feeling ill; an ideal such as:
*We don't want Daddy to be sick
do we?*

It was a complicated question,
like a mouse trap, for a child seeing
the day end just as it began,

as the hurdy-gurdy and the games,
the sweet, soft fried dough,
die away and Mom's car backs out

of the dusty field full of cars, each one
some kids who got to stay,
regular people.

The Younger Generation

When he says he loves me on the floor
  of the park
I feel the rough grass on my soft arms
  and long legs,

the July night like a cloud, a house
  of air enclosing
us in blue, the final minutes of the day.
  I love you too,

I say. It comes out of me like a cough,
  erupting
from my prison, the hard, familiar bars
  of my distrust,

though I swear my love is nothing like
  that uptight,
money-making generation; nor was there
  ever a July

like this, a greener lawn, or any tiger lilies,
  luxurious air,
lips like his, or dark brown curly hair.
  We don't taste

like gin—no, love! We can't think of them
  lying here like us
half naked, sweaty, with dirty feet
  from walking barefoot

through the dark and empty park
  surrounded by the sleeping
city. Soon it will arise,
  and cast us out.

We Skinny Kids

We skinny kids, we thought
we were Brando,
he was real.

I got on his motorcycle.
I wrapped my arms around him,
his old shirt.

He raced me over an open field
deep in Connecticut
in high summer.

We flew over centuries
of fakery, it was all bullshit
to us. I'll never laugh

like that again. Next day
Dad came out to get me,
a stranger, each to each.

My selfishness, he called it,
my inconsiderateness,
but it was worse than that.

Fear Is a Story

Fear is a story I tell myself,
  the imagined
outcome of imagined events,
  as if each time

I fall, or bleed, or weep, I protect
  my little pain,
keep it in a book to read later,
  to make sure

what cut me will cut me again.
  The first false
friend and liar becomes all men
  and hurricanes

churning in the Gulf, tornadoes,
  soon are on their way
to tear down my house and me away
  from home.

When the famous speaker ends his talk
  he begs
his audience for replies,
  yet we are silent,

reminded of our story about being
  stupid and losing
all our friends. We search for one
  who will raise

her voice and end the cramped silence
  in this place,
where nothing can harm us, no killers,
  no police.

The Red House, Late March

1. The Wrong Husband

How much misfortune precedes a bad marriage:
I was a girl hurrying from the Red House
to the woods and below to the pond,
jumping into the water, scorning my aunts
who lowered themselves in carefully
with little squeals. Then school. A dance.
A few drinks. A car taking the turns too fast.
Next I stood as white as the altar
vowing to live with the wrong husband.

I did and said things I regretted. Ages passed
and I didn't know how to Re-anything:
recover, repay, return, resume. Twenty-some
years. The house we called "Red" because it is
red (in one of the few direct observations
my family ever made) is quiet when I arrive
though the surrounding pines wave their branches
like great shaggy beasts and below them the pond
is piebald. I'm thinking I was mistaken
coming back when I turn and see my cousin Nate
walking up the worn drive, the image of my father,
and the old love seizes me. He used to row us out
to the middle of the pond and bait our lines,
a small lesson in patience and timing we never
learned well. We can't call up the fish; the fish
comes when it will. Today Nate welcomes me
as if I had been away a few days, that's all.

2. The Cocktail Hour

The windy afternoon blows back the years:
girl with a fish, girl at school, girl swinging
between the arms of the lawn chairs as Mom
and Dad talk with Nate and Dorothy
about relatives and money, blaming
those absent for everything from looking
exactly alike to alcoholism,

complaining about the heat, the rain, the car,
the post office, middle age. The clink
of their glasses, the dogs whining, impatient
for a walk, my father's cough as he lights
another cigarette—now sacred,
sublime quotidian. The waving pines.
Their soft floors. How I ran
across the yard and came to a dead stop
at my mother, leaned against her
or passed my hand over her hand.
Just to be sure, as she sat beside
the thick woods, the still, moss-colored pond.

3. The Pond

By midsummer the pond was warm and felt
like swimming in thick, green-black bathwater.
It glinted here and there with tiny stars and streams
of fractured sunlight. Sometimes, as I let myself
sink a little, tired from kicking and pulling
with my arms all the way from the dock
to the float, I'd feel a slimy length across
my leg and cry out, "Snake!" But the grown-ups
talking on the dock called back,
"It's just a reed, the tail of a lily pad.
There are no snakes," they cried.

They failed to convince me though by then
we had entered and returned safely
from many bodies of water, lakes and oceans,
rivers, pools. We had crossed on boats
and lept from diving boards. We had learned
to see under salt water and how to walk
on stony floors. I loved to swim and needed
to believe the calls from shore but the pond
was like no other body in its mossy solidity,
its gravity, and because we owned it,
it was ours.

The unseen monster crossed my leg
and clung to me as I kicked hard to free myself.
I climbed the ladder to the dock and lay
trembling from cold and fear in the sun,
pressing my cheek against the warm, worn
dry wood, listening to my family's voices
as they continued the endless conversation,
sitting with their drinks beside the piles of oars
and fishing rods, the orange life preservers,
the blue-green dragonflies darting back and forth
on the pond's surface, weightlessly.

4. The Endless Conversation

They were afraid to stop talking because
if they did they would have to see
what was happening underwater.
Feel the snake. After the first drink,
Dad was drunk. We pretended not to notice
and even offered him another.
Mother, her arm draped over the chair,
went on talking with Auntie Dot
about the awful things: illness, mistakes, divorces,
long train rides, ill-fitting clothes,
bad cooking, bad neighborhoods.
Beyond these lay all the things that could never
be said, waiting quietly like the pond,
like we imagine the dead, as souls
lingering with us.

5. The House

In 1921 it was an abandoned schoolhouse
on some 100 acres of land. I'm sure
my uncle bought it for a song. He and Dottie
turned the one-room school into the open
kitchen, scene of so many Thanksgivings
and Sunday dinners, the living room

with its view of the birches staggering
down to the pond. And here it stands
on my return one March afternoon,
fulfilling its mission to endure.

Nate is here, a son, and I, a daughter.
But the curse of buying and selling was uttered
long before. Nate's weathered face and bow-legged
walk show the effort of it. He can't bring back
our brothers, sisters, little cousins scattered
all over the country. He keeps inviting us
and a few come back like me. Some, I hear,
have turned mean. Some religious. Some
have moved to the west coast and others
refuse to stay in touch.

Yet after dinner, taking one of four paths
through the woods, I reach the pond and see
Dad on the dock as he was, not a ghost
but my love for him, his thinning black hair
combed back, sitting alone, cross-legged
on an aluminum chair and gazing
into the woods. He brings his cigarette
to his mouth, inhales deeply, lets the smoke
out in one burst. It circles, hangs in air,
the life of my father, and dissolves there.

Beaujolais

The glass shines, sits calmly at her place,
  its measure

topped off again—
  and again—

becomes an evening, a dateless
  month, a phrase

that repeats itself,
  regrets itself,

a friend who looks away, a mysterious
  hurt,

a mouthful of questions like:
  Is he there?

Because she's not really seeing.
  Events meld

like trees passing in a car window,
  gray, gray, green.

She's only hearing the surfaces of words,
  not the speaker

or their intent.
  Such misunderstandings

are the means to many unsought endings
  like hers, her empty glass

stained with her lipstick, sweating
  on the square napkin.

A Death in the Other House

When I pass by I can't help thinking
of you on the floor.

If I had known—
but we, neighbors, friends, all of us,
we don't step on each other's yards.
Our welcome mats are gestures to an ideal world,
a small town no one ever leaves, a Jimmy Stewart movie.
We'd like to be welcoming like that, the mats say,
but the door is locked.

So your horror burrowed,
a constant headache, a constant smile,
and you assumed, naturally, that I had never felt
like you and would complain about your parties on the side porch,
take your wine and beer away.

You began to think you were right about everything:
Life is This. It will never change.
Nobody cares, especially him. The kids
are better off without me. Ugly. Stupid. Jerk.

You forgot about Spring.
Mary Kelly's poppies lift their orange heads
without you; the air fills with the roar of mowers,
motorcycles stopped at the light below on Genesee Street.
You forgot about Violet, your two-year old neighbor,
yelling for her mother with new-found words.
All that is missing is you, your ghost on the floor,
now perfected, virtuous, right.

White August

Mostly I thought about cigarettes,
how many were left, the four times a day
I could smoke and how soon I could get out.

That July and August the weather was white.
A haze had fallen over the world
and in the haze

we, the locked up, listened for the keys
to ring in the nurse's hand, the sign
mid-morning had come, the opening

of Door 32, our passage to the pavilion
where I sat apart and smoked three Winstons
in 15 minutes; enough to get me through

a few paranoid chats, us
against them mutinies,
interrogations: What was I in for?

Staying behind in the ward never occurred to me;
not smoking never occurred to me.
I was able to lock myself up,

sit in the dayroom by the hour with my book
amidst a mix of disco, crow,
cats, mosquito, trees full of monkeys,

and read the same sentence 20 times
before its meaning spelled itself out, like tiles
on a Scrabble board,

and a new set of letters stood propped before me.
Although I admired the woman who ran away,
I stayed put.

It was scarier out there, the place I began to call
the other side.
Anyway they brought the woman back.

The Visitors

Stop by. I'll be polite
though I have no food or drink to offer,
just a public room, a chair, a cup of shame.

You wear your bright summer shirts,
your legs are tan. When you talk about jobs
and home repair, you laugh.

"Thank you," I want to say, "but you come
from the other side. It isn't like that here."
Here live the pale,

washed clean faces of the innocent
and the furious who are no longer with you,
your thoughts on Zen meditation

and carnations. Vases of them standing
on the counter at the nurses' station.
My visitors rise to go. I want so badly to ask,

"Who are you visiting? Is it me?
What do I look like? Tell me. It must be me
you love, or why would you come?"

Fearless Moral Inventory

The lie I dress in silks is the one
I tell myself and not my hundred excuses
for being late.

Such lateness tells a tale no matter how
my lies succeed (and I am always amazed
that they do),

for what else is it if not wanting to be there,
fear of being there, someone
not quite there.

The world accepts me as I present myself,
as I seem to be. If I give half, I get half.
If I'm not myself, I'm a shadow.

Soon no one expects me to show up.
Behind my door I make up a life.
I fill it with politics—

plans to save the world. I fill it
with victims, rebels, movie stars.
I read a lot of novels.

I fill the ashtray. I get drunk.
I let my lovers in for awhile; for awhile
the sex is real. The body may not lie

but it gets tired and it can stand outside itself.
It can only give what it can;
then more is required.

That's what I'm missing. The more.
I have reached the deepest shallows.
I have used up every dime.

And I can't die. I'm too lazy to shoot myself.
That is, I don't have a gun. And I don't know yet
if death is better than sitting with my sponsor

handing over my resentments,
telling my secrets, one leading to another,
trusting that I am only human in the end.

Finding My Way to Jesus

My father taught me the first false lesson:
Never ask for directions. Never reveal what you don't know.
Better to spend hours going the wrong way and end up
nowhere, the kids in tears, the wife giving the shoulder
as she stares at the alien hills and buildings.

My mother was more complicated. This was the second
false lesson: she knew everything but pretended she knew nothing.
She had a dirty mind but pretended she didn't.
She never stopped talking, which was the third false lesson:
silence is not golden, it's full of snakes, keep talking.

On Sundays she took us to worship the man-god
while Dad stayed home proclaiming his disbelief.
The fourth false lesson: he didn't go to hell, as predicted.
Nor did I for stealing pencils and candy at the drugstore
and lying about it. Jesus was, my mother said,
the son of the father and the cross was for love of us.
Yet when we returned home her anger was the same;
if I prayed it was the same. My Jesus was an absence,
and I pretty much forgot him until the following Sunday.

Then Dad said—and this was the fifth false lesson—
"I have never been a gambler or a poet." Finally he said,
"There is no such thing as a nervous breakdown."
Meaning we can make reality invisible.

Years later I am still finding my way. I write poetry. I often pass
three makeshift crosses in a field in New York. Unknowingly, I enter
a trance filled with scenes from my life and what seem like original ideas
but are not. I pray for my family. They were just trying
to grow up like me, earn a living, handle the technology.
Love is too small a word for it.

Amends

The memory of small betrayals is the worst:
not wanting to pay the old man who lent me
his pick-up;

a ready sarcasm; running out on a friend
for a friend with what I wanted; stealing from
the drug store, my aunt;

Lula, Millie, Ann, all the women in hotels
who made my bed and cleaned my sink; all those
I made invisible

in stores, on trains, in the waiting room.
I am lodged in their stories, one of many careless
people in a hurry.

But the grand betrayals of lovers, mothers, children,
self, the ones we cannot speak of, ground
in the mortar of our history,

therefore easier, duller, having been endured—
I don't need to write them down; I was sorry, sorry,
but I stayed

drunk, refusing the mercy that pre-exists us all,
so pleased, so puffed up with the idea that I was
unforgivable. This

was my power. Who would care, who would
believe me, who would I be if I were not this
ratty victim?

Much easier to put my rudeness to the old man
behind me, to apologize to him, to a stranger,
than to my father.

Amends 2

More and more the past is like a dream,
like a long drive with a crazy friend
who stops where she wants,

speeds off, makes of partying
a marriage, of a marriage a week;
returns home

to a patient brother, a night's sleep
in the back bedroom, a few hurried stories
and it's off again. Then

when thrills grow tedious and she runs
into the new empty, she fills it
with a child

but all it does is cry: the shock of needs
not her own. We think we're sane,
but we're not.

The past was not a dream; it is
a history, and when I unroll the sheets
of time, hundreds

of notches appear in the line, each standing
for a chance, an opening among friends
and the beloved

to connect. I remember turning away,
the logic of my resentment—
hurting back

for hurt received. They say it isn't too late;
that seeing and believing are enough
even for the dead.

The Sacred Tables

Where there is privacy in bathrooms, hallways,
　even at Rite-Aid
in Aisle 3, my cart overflowing, I pray.
　Dear Goddess:

How You love my poverty-stricken thanks,
　my new listening
at small, battered tables and tucked-away booths
　to daughters

who did drugs with their parents; bought heroin
　for their fathers;
daughters too afraid to leave behind the corpse
　of their marriages;

who lost their children; who insist they hate
　their mothers.
Imagine hating your mother, what that is
　really about.

Today I'm waiting with a cup of strong coffee
　at Domenico's
for Maria, a daughter I met at the Tuesday
　eight o'clock meeting.

She is almost always late but her tears come
　fast, as if
she's been waiting all day to talk, years.
　Her tears come

and go, a film over her eyes, a wash,
　and sometimes
they glitter deep in the corner, tiny gems,
　pieces of her.

As Fran T. and Caroline once sat with me,
I sit with Maria.
Like me she apologizes. For being.
For all of it.

Shakes her head when I ask how it's going.
"Fine. Ok."
Like me she waits for proof it works, this
reaching out shit.

Years of abstinence have made me
suspiciously clean
and clear-eyed. Dressed. Not lonely-looking.
Uncool.

Only two things recommend me:
No one makes up
a story like mine. And when Maria asked
if we could meet

I said yes. I am here. At the sacred tables
where the extra-
ordinary happens—gently, invisibly—more
than you'd think.

Slowly the words come, mazy and mixed up,
hoarse, in a rush
of fright, crazy ideas, bitter resentment.
and fill the space

across the table where no one exists except
us, where thousands
of secrets live and die. "Hey," I ask again,
"what's going on?"

Cindy Day has published in the *Green Mountains Review, Southern Poetry Review, Nine Mile,* and *The Healing Muse,* among other magazines. Four of her poems appear in *Last Call: Poems of Alcoholism, Addiction and Deliverance,* edited by Sarah Gorham & Jeffrey Skinner, Sarabande Books, 1997. In 2008 she won the Emerging Poet Award from Stone Canoe Magazine, Syracuse University. Most recently she participated in the PRO program at the Downtown Writer's Center in Syracuse, NY.

A native of Hartford, Connecticut and a graduate of the University of Hartford, she has lived and worked in Central New York since 1974. Since the age of 16, writing, primarily poetry, has been at the center of her life. She has also worked in retail, as an office administrator for a nonprofit and in medical offices. She has written and edited three area newsletters, and has been involved in her community for many years as a volunteer for such organizations as Hospice, the Utica Public Library and AA and Al Anon. Currently, she serves on the board for The Center for Family Life & Recovery in Utica, New York, where she lives with her husband.

www.ingramcontent.com/pod-product-compliance
Lightning Source LLC
LaVergne TN
LVHW040117080426
835507LV00041B/1354